TEACHING
IN
MAGENTA

TEACHING
IN
MAGENTA

100 PATHS TO JOY AND WELL-BEING
FOR YOU AND YOUR STUDENTS

James Alan Sturtevant

ILLUSTRATED BY **Lauren Barnes**

These books are available at special discounts when purchased in
quantity for premiums, promotions, fundraising, and educational
use. For inquiries and details, contact us at 10Publications.com.

Published by Times 10
Highland Heights, OH
10Publications.com

Cover and Interior Design by Steven Plummer
Editing by Carrie White-Parrish
Copyediting by Jennifer Jas

Library of Congress Cataloging-in-Publication Data is available.

ISBN (paperback): 978-1-948212-24-3
ISBN (eBook): 978-1-948212-59-5
First Printing: July, 2020

I'm sentimental about magenta. I love the way it looks, and I love what it represents. I'm compelled to add one more attribute to magenta's noble inventory—joy. When I gaze at the color magenta, I feel joy. My mom's name is Joy. She passed away in August of 2015. I thought about her often as I wrote these words, and I felt profound joy. This book is dedicated to her sweet memory.

TABLE OF CONTENTS

Section 2: Magenta Teachers Embrace Optimism

Section 3: Magenta Teachers Pursue Balance

Section 4: Magenta Teachers Adapt

Section 5: Magenta Teachers Find Contentment

PREFACE

EARLY MARCH OF 2019 represented a typical Central Ohio late winter for me. I was gearing up to coach track and field, which was about to start, and feeling the siren song of spring break at month's end. Then, quite unexpectedly, my school district offered a buyout to older teachers.

Now, I'd navigated thirty-four years in the classroom. I knew that retirement was near, but I had planned to go a few more years. I still loved the job. But the buyout was significant, and I knew I had to take the offer seriously. I also knew that there was no way I could leave teaching unless I could replace the multitude of daily social interactions with students and colleagues. Fortunately, a local university offered me an adjunct position teaching future teachers. I also forged a relationship with a local aid agency that wanted me to help refugees learn English and pass their citizenship test.

With these future social interaction opportunities

secured, I decided to take my school district up on their offer. My life fundamentally changed that March.

When spring break rolled around at the end of the month, I had set the wheels of change in motion, and I was in a bit of a tizzy. *Wow. I can't believe I'm doing this. Wait. Should I be doing this? Yes. This is an extraordinary opportunity to say goodbye to my wonderful K–12 students, but continue to bond with students by teaching at the college level.*

Regardless of that change, I knew one thing: I would utilize my greatest strength, which is my disposition, as I moved forward. I am a positive guy. Students and colleagues embrace this and frequently point it out to me. Some accuse me of being lucky for having such an outlook, but those who make such claims don't know me well. My successful disposition is a product of design, not fate. I've experienced life's hardships, like anyone who's lived as long as I have. I've experienced many days when I could barely face my students. But I made the decision early in my career that I was going to *create* awesome days. Sometimes, this took much effort, but the adage "Fake it till you make it" somehow worked for me. I certainly don't have a

100 percent success rate, but most days, when I set my mind to improve them, turn out great.

I'm a big fan of taking that ownership. I encourage more people to do it.

With that in mind, on that dreamy spring break of 2019 as I reflected on my career and future educational endeavors, I experienced a powerful eureka moment. I decided to share exactly *how* I created those outstanding days. That idea inspired this book. I started typing, amazed at how my fingers magically flew over the keys on my laptop. By the end of April, I was done with the manuscript. I'd never written anything so effortlessly.

I felt that 2019 was perfect timing for publishing a book on teacher well-being. I noticed more empathetic signals from administrators. They seemed to recognize that pushing too hard was counterproductive, and that the Law of Diminishing Returns also applied to teachers. I was hoping for a 2019 copyright, which seemed like good timing for a book that would help teachers (and their students) find more bliss.

However, publishing books frequently takes longer than you think.

Then, the coronavirus struck. Book publishing was put on hold, and I, like most educators, started dealing with the variable-laden challenge of online teaching in a COVID-19-stricken world. Such monumental events alter trajectories. While students and classrooms still existed, schools were inevitably different. Instruction was different, too. We, the teachers, became different.

But perhaps, I thought, we could be different in a positive way.

In short, COVID-19 itself, and the quarantine that followed, made me feel even more strongly about the importance of this book in the educational world. Yes, this world requires that we make adjustments. Take ownership of our days. Become a beacon of teacher well-being. Become a rock to our students, colleagues, and parents. They need us. This book will show you how to fulfill those promises. Teachers tirelessly promote the idea that students must embrace a growth mindset. This book is your opportunity to practice what you preach by building better tomorrows—for yourself and your students. It's one thing to have a goal to create a better classroom environment. It's quite another to have a detailed plan. This book will provide exactly that.

INTRODUCTION
WHY MAGENTA?

MAGENTA IS A versatile color. Sometimes it's described as purplish-red, and at other times, mauvish-crimson. It's distinctive. It's bold. I love it!

I grew up and even went to college surrounded by magenta. My father was a professor at Muskingum University, a small liberal arts school in Southeastern Ohio, and I graduated from there. Muskingum's colors are black and magenta, which is a courageous combo.

My devotion to magenta, however, isn't based primarily on school allegiance or its inherent beauty; it's because this color inspires virtue. If you research its meaning, you'll find a slew of noble qualities. I love the description of magenta's noble nature on empower-yourself-with-color-psychology.com. This book will focus on five qualities you can find in that narrative:

- Compassion
- Optimism

- Balance

- Adaptability

- Contentment

Each section of this book focuses on translating and inserting one of these magenta attributes into your classroom. Manifesting these attributes in concert will bring joy to your classroom and your professional life.

Every teacher can find joy and well-being for themselves and their students if teaching in magenta is their daily goal. In the following pages, you'll find one hundred powerful paths, gleaned from over three decades of teaching, that lead to teaching in magenta. I've been astounded by how these ideas flowed from my heart to my fingertips.

How to Use This Book

Teaching in Magenta is meant to be consumed slowly. Think of it as a journey of discovery, with one hundred different paths or options to explore. If you rush through the pages and look for the fastest route to the end, magenta could become elusive, and you'll miss some marvelous experiences and beautiful scenery.

Speaking of scenery, as you experience the paths of *Teaching in Magenta*, you'll encounter a few sketches during your journey. In the tradition of my Hacking Engagement podcast, which features students as guests, I've enlisted the help of a young lady to take the magenta journey and share her feelings through her favorite medium. Lauren Barnes is a high school student and budding artist. As she read this book, she put pencil to paper. Her interpretations of the paths are scattered throughout the book, in no particular order. They appear without labels or captions, so you can interpret them as you see fit. The images amplify ideas and encourage nuanced interpretations. Also, what's a book without pictures? I'm glad her voice is present in this book. Thanks, Lauren!

At this point, you might be thinking that one hundred unique paths are a lot to explore. Take your time and allow this adventure to unfold over a nine-week grading period, or perhaps a semester. You don't have to read this book in a linear fashion. Aim to read just a page or two each day to inspire you to create some magenta in your classroom.

This is not a bedtime story. It's more of a sunrise

story. Keep it on your desk at school and read a page before first period. Or store it in the kitchen and read a page during breakfast. Reading a page will only take a few minutes, but the impact on you and your students could be eternal.

SECTION 1

MAGENTA TEACHERS SHOW COMPASSION

COMPASSION IS POWER. Some associate power with the victors, the ultra-competitive, the publicity seekers, the sarcastic, the masters of Machiavellian tactics ... the people we celebrate in contemporary society. Such individuals are often considered virile and heroic, but these strivers are frequently motivated by anxiety, not strength.

Compassionate teachers are the opposite. They're secure in their skin. They give. They reach out. They manage their emotions. They risk ridicule. They don't seek self-promotion. Become *that* kind of powerful educator. Meander through the paths in this section and get inspired to rescue youngsters with your compassion rather than anxiety or competition.

1

APOLOGIZE

APOLOGIES ARE POWERFUL, but how often do you apologize to students? Perhaps you got frustrated yesterday and raised your voice in a kid's direction. Or you were too aggressive with a reprimand. The target of your wrath may have only partially inspired your emotions in that moment. You may have been mad at your spouse or a colleague, or you are harboring frustration from the previous period's behavior. Today, apologize to any kids who absorbed your outburst. You could pull them aside in the hall before they enter class, or—and this takes courage but has great power—apologize to them in front of the class. "Maria, I came on too strong at you yesterday. I'm sorry. I care about you! I shouldn't have done that."

2

PUMP THE BREAKS

SARCASM SEEMS HARMLESS. You make a joke at another's expense. If you have a close relationship with your target, they might not mind; they may even enjoy the barb. But limit sarcasm in the classroom, particularly if the teacher is the one who's doing the dishing. Remember, this tactic involves making the target look bad. This is not the atmosphere you want to foster. Humor in the classroom, or in life in general, is wonderful. But today, refrain from making that sarcastic statement on the tip of your tongue. Instead, see if there's a more positive way to insert levity.

3

REACH BACK

YOU PARADE INTO class amped for the day's lesson. You launch into your sales pitch, but you become discouraged when you notice that a student is not listening to your enthusiastic introduction. Instead, she is looking down at her phone and consuming a social media post. The post she's reading is just as interesting to her as the Taiping Rebellion is to you. Stay encouraged and amped up. You were young once, too. Granted, you may have been a highly motivated youngster, but you no doubt had plenty of distracted friends. Today, just be cool and remember your youth. You have the opportunity to influence this student, and your efforts will be more fruitful if they come from a place of acceptance rather than anger.

4

PREPARE FOR THE QUESTION

TEACHERS GENERALLY DISLIKE hearing, "Why do we have to learn this?" It often seems like the questioner is attempting to throw cold water on your lesson. It's understandable for a teacher to get frustrated by this prompt, but today, welcome the prompt as an opportunity. When you think about it, it's a perfectly fair and legitimate question. So go ahead and prepare an outstanding response. Craft such a marvelous response that you provide it to students whether or not they ask the question. Rather than getting upset about the question and overreacting, be prepared to answer it daily.

5

GET MOVING

WHEN OFFICE ENVIRONMENTS are portrayed in movies and on television, working at a desk or in a cubicle is scorned. And yet, it's exactly what we require students to do every day. Today, break this negative norm. Sure, you might be confined to a small classroom populated with lots of bodies, but that doesn't matter. Get your kids up and moving. Perhaps they rotate through stations. It could be that they perform a skit. Maybe they get collaboration appointments with classmates. Perhaps they exit the room and go on a QR code scavenger hunt. Or it could be that the kids must come up to your desk and retrieve their handouts. Get those youngsters moving. Don't allow your room to look like another scorned workplace in a sitcom.

6

BRING THE HEAT

I USHER 150 guests (my students) into my home (my classroom) daily. I want my guests to feel welcome. A great way to do this is to exercise enthusiastic hospitality. If one of your guests needs a tissue, pull one out of the box and jog it over. If they need a pencil, hand-deliver it. When my mom passed away, my wife and I were cleaning out her house and found a small electric heater that she always kept beside her. I now keep it in my room because my school is generally freezing. I told my students that when I turn it on, I feel like my mom is giving me a hug. That elicited a loud "aw" from my kids. I got an even bigger reaction when I unplugged it, marched it back to a shivering young lady, plugged it back in, turned it on, and aimed it in her direction. Treat your kids like treasured guests.

7

NIX NOSTALGIA

BEING NOSTALGIC IS perfectly understandable. You probably remember a time when you were younger and more vibrant, and the future was bright. Nostalgia, however, is not objective. I adore the memories of my youth, but society subscribed to many horrific norms during those days. Today, instead of wishing your students were more like you and your contemporaries when you were young, remember that the past ways of life are not as good as they seem, and also acknowledge that they're not coming back. Such thoughts separate you from modern youth. Your students are citizens of the present. Accept this and be relevant.

8

REASSURE A ROOKIE

DO YOU REMEMBER your first year in the classroom? You probably felt inadequate. Sometimes, I think about my rookie year and wonder how those poor kids learned anything. On top of a first-year teacher's concerns about classroom management, lesson plans, and the need to include parental contact, I dealt with significant anxiety over whether my contract would get renewed. Today, reach out to a rookie on your staff. Tell them a story about how stressful your first year was, and then reassure them that you're there for them. Tell them how much easier their sophomore year will be. And finally, ask how they're doing and be prepared to listen.

9

VENERATE A VETERAN

ONE NEGATIVE ASPECT of aging is the feeling that you're losing relevance. I'm fortunate in that younger teachers sometimes reach out to me for guidance. When they do, it makes me feel awesome. I try to give them solid advice, and many are grateful. What they don't realize is how energizing it is for me when they ask. Today, seek out an older colleague and pay them a compliment or ask for advice. You'll be doing them (and you) a great service, and they just may give you a wonderful suggestion.

10

LISTEN WITH YOUR FEET

MY PRINCIPAL IS constantly in demand. He once rushed breathlessly into my class to inform me about something. I used the poor guy as a prop to demonstrate my fascination with nonverbal communication. After he hurriedly delivered his message, I asked him to freeze and remain still. Remarkably, he did. I then directed my students to look at Mr. Jados's feet, which he pointed toward the door. I informed them, "Mr. Jados is anxious to leave us and get to his next appointment. The feet don't lie. They indicate exactly where the body wants to go. Thanks for cooperating, Mr. Jados." Today, when you interact with students, point your feet directly at them, and give them your full attention. You'll communicate volumes before you utter your first word.

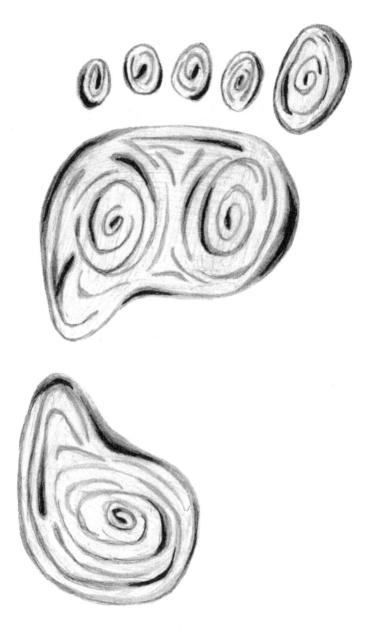

11

SMILE

EARLY IN MY tenure as a presenter, I conducted a PD session that I felt went okay, but I didn't bond with my audience as I'd hoped. After the session, I did a postmortem. I generally bond easily with folks. What was missing? I then recalled my first year of teaching. My department chair approached me about a week after school started and said, "You're actually a gregarious guy. In your job interview, you were as serious as a heart attack. I didn't think you had a humorous bone in your body." I was shocked by this revelation and became conscious of making better first impressions. Before my next PD presentation opportunity, I recalled that interaction with my department chair and then made certain to unleash my gregarious nature. I smiled at my audience frequently, and we bonded. Today, make sure you start each interaction with a big smile.

12

SPREAD THE LOVE

IT'S ESSENTIAL TO tell kids you love them after you reprimand them. It's important to tell kids you love them if you just realized that you didn't give them your full attention. This simple and powerful act was modeled to me by Steve Kokovich, my old college education professor. I used to stop by his office to talk—which, when I look back on it, was pretty obtrusive of me. One day, I stopped to talk, and he was in crisis mode. He told me, "Sorry, young man, I can't talk at the moment," and spun back toward his desk. I totally got it and turned to leave. And yet, he must have felt bad because he called out over his shoulder, "You know I love you, Jimmy." I'll never forget that. Today, tell your kids you love them.

13

DROP THE BATON

IT'S VITALLY IMPORTANT to empathize with kids. A great way to do this is to tell a story about when you were young. Occasionally, you can recount heroic exploits where you hit the walk-off home run in the bottom of the ninth, or when you came close to curing cancer in tenth grade biology. But today, tell a story about when you faced a hardship. It could be when you asked a girl to homecoming and got rejected, or when you dropped the relay baton at the state track meet (I actually did this). Let kids know that they aren't alone in their struggles and that you're a sympathetic ear if they need one.

14

ASK FOR DATING ADVICE

WHEN YOU ASK someone for their opinion, it's a sign of respect. You have a daily opportunity to show students you respect them by asking for their help. A fun and low-risk way to demonstrate this trust is to ask for suggestions on where to take your lovely wife or husband to dinner for your upcoming date night. Through just such an inquiry, my wife and I found our favorite Chinese restaurant. Thanks, kids! Today, seek advice from students. It could be something low risk like a restaurant review. Your students will feel respected, and you just may find your new favorite restaurant.

15

EXECUTE A SUBTLE COURSE CORRECTION

WHEN YOU WORK with 150 people for 180 days straight, there's going to be tension. Sometimes, your most reliable and enthusiastic students stop producing and become standoffish. Sometimes your problematic kids become more obstinate. Today, while you're stationed by your door greeting kids as they enter class, execute a subtle course correction with a student who strayed. Pull them aside and ask them to join you in leaning against the door and greeting peers, and then just talk to the youngster. Ask them if everything is okay. Apologize if you've gotten frustrated with them in front of their peers. But most importantly, tell them you care about them and that you're there for them. It's amazing how often this simple tactic works.

16

CONTROL YOUR WELTANSCHAUUNG

WELTANSCHAUUNG **MEANS WORLDVIEW.** It's one of the few German words I know. When I conduct PD sessions for teachers, I prompt the audience to stand if they were in the National Honor Society, which results in a lot of standing audience members. Next, I ask those who played a varsity sport and those who graduated from high school with at least a 3.00 GPA to join the Honor Society folks in standing. At this point, I congratulate the few who remain in their seats. "You have a distinct advantage to bond with a lot of kids," I tell them. Remember, many students at your school will never achieve any of the things I asked about. Their *weltanschauung* is different from yours. They may not look at school in the same positive light as you did. Today, embrace those kids who aren't going to have many group photos in the yearbook.

17

LOWER THE TEMPERATURE

WHEN PEOPLE ARE angry, their volume typically elevates; they tend to get flushed, and they often become animated and demonstrative. They absolutely stop listening. If they confront another who's also angry, they can feed off their adversary's destructive energy and get even more frustrated. In extreme cases, confrontations can get physical. Your job as a teacher is to lower the thermostat. Today, be a calming presence in a volatile confrontation. Be prepared for others to redirect daggers toward you, but don't let those attacks change your demeanor. Just keep calming and keep reassuring. By reducing conflict, you will model resolution strategies that students may copy for decades. That would be a marvelous achievement.

18

DON'T GET BUCKY

MY MOTHER USED to utter this odd command at my siblings and me. It meant "Attitude adjustment, pronto!" Guess what? Teachers tend to get a little bucky near the end of a semester. Everyone is anxious for a little R & R, and the classroom routine tends to get stale. My wife used to say, "You're not as fun to be around in May." I always struggled with the frustrations I'd had with students the entire semester, like procrastinating on projects, which became acute near the end of the term. But it wasn't fair for me to get bucky near the end. The students were just doing what they'd always done. They were being consistent. I wasn't. The next time you find yourself in a similar situation, remember my mom's command, and keep it fresh instead of bucky. Whatever is flustering you, change it by next semester, and preserve your relationship with your current crop of kids.

19

RECOGNIZE THAT YOU HAVE COMPANY

MY FATHER WAS a history professor at Muskingum University for forty-six years. He loved his job. He inspired me to become a teacher, too. At the college level, he didn't have to contend with classroom management. His clientele was highly motivated, he engaged with advanced content, and his daily schedule and academic calendar were the stuff of dreams. When I told my dad that I was going to become a teacher, he was overjoyed. He spoke of his love of the profession and how it was a great path for me. But he did issue a warning. "Jim, 95 percent of the time I love going to school, but there are days where I can barely face them." Today, understand that the anxiety about facing students is universal. You have plenty of company. Once you've internalized this mantra, become an evangelist and reassure a colleague who's dreading going to their next period.

20

NURTURE CONFIDENCE

I WAS A wreck my first few weeks of college. I studied and studied for my first exam and ended up with a 70 percent. I nearly dropped out. I had no confidence. But a few kind words from a professor made all the difference. "Relax, Jim. You're intelligent. You just have to develop your own method of studying. Once you do that, you'll spend less time and study more effectively." That simple pep talk gave me the confidence to continue and eventually thrive. Today, have a conversation like that with a student who's struggling. You just may rescue their future.

SECTION 2

MAGENTA TEACHERS EMBRACE OPTIMISM

OPTIMISM TRANSFORMS MUNDANE tasks into rapid checks on a to-do list. When you're excited about the future, you don't get bogged down in tedious chores. I remember my excitement as a child when I glanced over my shoulder during dinner and caught a thrilling glimpse of the dessert my mom had crafted just waiting for me on the kitchen counter. I made quick work of my vegetables to be permitted to indulge in sweet caloric bliss. This section will help you cope with not only mundane obligations so you can get to that dessert, but also with profound setbacks. Teaching is full of those, but please don't be negative in front of kids. Whatever you're struggling with isn't their fault. Students enjoy optimistic teachers. They're fun to be around. They're cheesy, in a good way. Keep reminding students and yourself that there are magnificent desserts on the horizon once you clear a few hurdles.

21

BOUNCE BACK

RECENTLY, YOU HAD a rough day. You had high hopes for your lesson, and it ended up being a dud. Your high-maintenance students were disruptive and wallowed in drama. You felt like a failure. You couldn't wait to see the school in your rearview mirror as you exited the staff parking lot. No worries. Every teacher has these days. Today, however, is a new day. You don't have to create the best day ever, just a better day. The school year is a marathon, not a sprint. Good days are in your future. Your students aren't obsessing over yesterday, so why are you? Go to school and have a better day.

22

SOMETIMES, PREACH TO THE CHOIR

THE CLICHÉ ABOUT preaching to the choir is generally used to mean: don't do it; you're wasting your breath; focus your efforts instead on targets that need to hear your message. But just maybe, the choir desperately needs to be preached to as well. Today, share with your students, whether you think they need the message or not. Go ahead and extol the virtues of treating peers with compassion, giving a solid academic effort, and striving to be good citizens of the school. You'll be praising and reinforcing outstanding behaviors. You may also be converting, through osmosis, students who have the potential to become wonderful kids but still are reluctant to make that leap.

23

BE A BEACON

MOTIVATED CHURCHGOERS GENERALLY revel in the sermon, where the clergy's message confirms and expands upon their convictions. However, for the reluctant parishioners, the sermon can be a counterproductive drudgery. Classrooms are similar. You typically have a cadre of confident and motivated learners, and unfortunately, a contingent of the opposite. Today, be cognizant of your reluctant learners. Be careful about launching into any sermons that may be counterproductive. Instead, demonstrate to each student you interact with, and their peers, a compassion, empathy, and commitment to learning. Leading by example will transform you into a beacon of light for students lost at sea.

52

24

TRUST

LAST CHRISTMAS, MY lovely daughter-in-law, Niki, gifted me *How to Walk* by Thich Nhat Hanh. This short book consists of about ninety suggestions on how to walk meditatively. Each suggestion or page is roughly one hundred words. Sound familiar? I forgot about her transformational gift until one March day when I saw it and started to read it, and now I read a page daily. Niki's wonderful present didn't make a huge impact when I opened the wrapping paper, but its influence grew. Your students, especially your stand-offish students, are similar to me with my Christmas gift. Aim to be patient, and realize that you may be impacting and influencing them over time. I've had former students rave about my class, but while I was teaching them, I didn't think they even liked me. Be optimistic and trust the future. You may not realize the fruits of today's efforts until down the line.

25

LEARN SOMETHING

AUTHOR RICHARD BACH crafted a beautiful quote about teaching: "We teach best what we most need to learn." I teach world civilization, and we navigate through an entire unit on Buddhism. A key ingredient in Buddhism is mindfulness. Your humble narrator runs at a high octane, and I became fascinated with meditation the first time I taught this unit. I started meditating, and I've done it ever since. I shared my new passion with students by including a mindfulness activity. I've received gobs of positive comments. Today, broadcast a personal lesson you've learned from the unit you're studying. Demonstrate optimism and a growth mindset by unveiling ways that today's lesson can enrich students' lives, and yours.

26

SERVE APPETIZERS

INSTEAD OF LAUNCHING into your lesson and presenting immediately, tease your students first. Get them excited about diving into the lesson. The same tactic that the local cinema used on you and your partner last Saturday during date night will work in your classroom. The theater displayed an engaging trailer that you both agreed looked irresistible. Today, before you dive into a topic like the Sepoy Rebellion, for example, prompt kids to collaborate on the impact of a rumor. A rumor sparked the rebellion. Great hooks create instant relevancy. When students learn about the Sepoy Rebellion, they'll think of the impact of rumors on their lives. Hook your kids, and create a much more receptive audience that's open to learning. The more excited they are, the more optimistic the entire experience will become.

27

COMPLIMENT THE CRABBY

WHEN YOU'RE ANGRY and preparing to confront someone and launch into your diatribe, it takes the wind out of your sails when they unexpectedly deflate you by saying something like, "Hello! It's so good to see you. I love your shirt." It's hard to maintain your edge when someone pays you a compliment. Today, diffuse a student who's frustrated with you. Before they have the chance to spread their gloom, say something like, "Man, you're getting tall," or "I loved what you wrote in your essay." Give a crabby kid a compliment, and watch their animosity fade.

28

FAKE IT TILL YOU MAKE IT

OF COURSE, SOME days you just don't feel like going to school. Such emotions often materialize on Monday mornings. And if you feel this way, think about your poor students. At least you get a paycheck for being there. So today, put on a happy face. Greet students enthusiastically. Bound into class, ready to roll. Say cheesy things like, "Today has great potential," or "Don't be in a rush to get to the weekend. You could miss something awesome that could happen to you today." You may consider this act a bit fake, but it's a harmless performance. I do it all the time and find that it generally becomes a self-fulfilling prophecy.

29

TAKE A RISK

WHEN I WATCHED a biography of Jeff Bezos, the founder of Amazon, I was struck by how one of his early bosses complimented him on how he kept producing ideas—ideas that Jeff thought were impractical, but still worth articulating. Today, encourage students to take those kinds of risks. Many kids are afraid to speak up because they don't want to look stupid. Take away that fear by introducing anonymity. Challenge kids to speculate, and then offer them the option to do it incognito with Google Forms or Pear Deck or Peergrade or Plickers, or any other platform that allows for anonymous expression. You may inspire an innovator who will change the planet.

30

DRINK A LARGE GLASS OF WATER

I LOVE TO share my life with my kids. It makes me so much more approachable. I particularly like sharing odd things I do, and for a great impact, you cannot beat a live demonstration. I display my water-drinking fetish by chugging a large glass of water in front of my class. They think the performance is strange, but they watch attentively and then generally ask a lot of questions. I love that my kids get to know me better, and I feel good about exposing them to positive ideas. Drinking water is good for you. Today, demonstrate something you do that could enrich your kids' lives. If you drink a large glass of water, be prepared to visit the restroom at the end of the period!

31

CLEAR THE DECK

FORMER NAVY SEAL Admiral William H. McRaven delivered a marvelous graduation speech at the University of Texas in 2014. His commencement address became an internet sensation and was transformed into a popular book, *Make Your Bed*. Admiral McRaven pointed out that when you perform this task in the morning, even if you end up having a miserable day, you at least come home to a nicely made bed. Before heading home today, tidy up your desk. No matter what tomorrow brings, at least you'll be greeted by a clean desk in the morning.

32

SWITCH ROLES

I'M AN ADULT! I'm the expert! Listen to me! Never say such things. Even if you don't say such obnoxious things, try not to even *think* them. The internet is the great education equalizer. Information on virtually any topic is a click away. Educators are no longer the gatekeepers of knowledge. After you deliver today's prompt, shock your kids by saying, "Teach me something!" Challenge them to go deeper. Inspire them to impress and enlighten you. There's incredible power in that bit of humility on your part, and it firmly declares confidence in your kids.

33

MORPH EXPECTATIONS

"I'VE BEEN THROUGH some terrible things in my life, some of which actually happened." This marvelous quote from Mark Twain seems like it was written especially for teachers. When you have challenging classes and challenging students, you might find yourself ruminating all evening about what bad things might happen tomorrow. If you get yourself too fussed up, the next day could be a self-fulfilling prophecy. Today, embrace Mark Twain's quote. A lot of bad things are purely the product of your imagination. Relax and give your kids a chance.

34

REMEMBER THAT THIS TOO SHALL PASS

ONE SEMESTER A few decades ago, I taught a class from hell. I remember thinking, *How in the world do I survive this semester?* Oddly, I don't remember many specifics about that crew of students. A few blurry faces and perhaps a name or two are all I can salvage. This class caused me so much grief then, but now it is a distant, fuzzy memory. Remember this story today as you walk into your high-maintenance class. One day, they'll be a distant memory, too.

35

PRACTICE WET BLANKET MANAGEMENT

KIDS ARE A tough audience. During your passionate lesson delivery, you can see individuals staring at their phones, playing absurd games on their Chromebooks, putting their heads down, and not displaying engaged body language. That's frustrating. You also may have a cantankerous kid challenging the legitimacy of the lesson. Today, don't let this fuss you up. Remember that these disengaged kids don't speak and act for everyone. These students may also have additional variables brewing in their lives that impact their behavior and have nothing to do with your lesson. Don't obsess over your wet blankets. Focus on the majority of your students who are engaged and receptive.

36

MEND A FENCE

A FEW YEARS ago, an administrator in my district leveled a tough decision in a Machiavellian fashion to a person I care deeply about. I was angry. I vowed to steer clear of the culprit because I didn't trust my emotions. When they came up in conversation or when I'd see them present at district events, I'd get all stirred up. Last December, I developed a strong urge to contact them. I wrote to them and proclaimed that while I disagreed with their decision and the way they executed it, I forgave them, and I was moving on. They were in my room within twenty-four hours, expressing relief and gratitude. It felt so good to let go of this burden. Today, reach out to the person with whom you've had a conflict. Mend that fence and relieve yourself of a burden.

37

EVOLVE

WHEN I'M CONTRACTED to conduct PD, I enjoy facilitating breakout sessions because they give me a chance to interact with teachers one-on-one or in small groups. Schools bring me in to encourage staff to evolve, both in terms of their interactions with kids and with their instructional techniques. Some teachers get frustrated when they are encouraged to change. That's understandable. They often make statements such as, "I teach the way I was taught, and it worked for me" or "I've been teaching this way for over a decade. Why should I change?" These comments are fear-based. Don't be afraid. When we embrace evolution, we remain relevant. The world changes. Be supple and thrive.

38

ANTICIPATE TOMORROW

I HAVE A lot more yesterdays than tomorrows. My students have a lot more tomorrows than yesterdays. I'm envious. I believe I'm going to miss some neat stuff. My students frequently compliment me on my optimism, and I understand why they appreciate it because it's a drag being around complainers. Today, make sure that you aren't a drag. When teachers complain about where the world is heading, they don't understand that students are going to spend a lot more time in the future than the teachers are. Avoid poisoning the well. Be excited for students and their futures, and make it clear that you wish you could tag along. They'll be grateful and may become more optimistic, too.

39

DROP YOUR SHOULDERS

I CANNOT RECALL interacting with anyone who suffered from anxiety or depression and who had magnificent posture. The opposite was often true. Think of this observation the next time you wish you were somewhere else as you walk into school. Try this experiment. Greet each class with a smile and incredible posture. Before it's showtime, rotate your shoulders and drop them away from your ears. Lengthen your neck, suck in that gut, and smile. Your students might wonder if you had a glass of cabernet between periods. Let them think that. Just enjoy the optimistic billboard that you've become. You may have a magnificent day all because of your little experiment.

40

TAKE INVENTORY

MOST DAYS, BOTH positive and negative things happen to you. Acknowledging that simple phenomenon is an important step. Unfortunately, negative experiences seem to deliver more impact. It could be a confrontation or a critical comment from a student, a parent, or your principal. Or, it could be something more nuanced, such as having had high hopes for a lesson that didn't end up engaging your kids. Regardless, during the day, many subtle positives materialize that you don't fully acknowledge. Today, take stock of the colleague who asks about your family, the student who completes her assignment for the first time in weeks, and the kid who you thought didn't like you, yet he gave you a smile. If you do this regularly, you might find yourself smiling more often as well.

SECTION 3

MAGENTA TEACHERS PURSUE BALANCE

PRETEND THAT YOU'RE a boat in distress, stranded in the middle of the ocean and tossed back and forth and up and down by a violent storm. Life can certainly be like that. But it's reassuring to have a stable captain at the helm, guiding the vessel and calming the passengers. This section will help you become like that brave captain navigating life's treacherous waters, a magnificent accomplishment in its own right. Obtaining balance can also be a marvelous gift to your students. You could become a calm Polaris to kids, many of whom experience typhoons as they circumvent adolescence.

41

REMAIN CALM

IN MY SOCIAL Studies Department, we frequently ask each other, "How's your supplemental class?" This is the ultra-challenging class for which you probably deserve extra pay for facing each day. We all have classes like this. How about today taking deep breaths and repeating an affirmation before you wade in? *It's just one class, and it's just one period. Every teacher in every school has a supplemental class. I have plenty of company, and I'll be fine. I will eventually bond with these kids, and that will be wonderful for them and me.* Determine to manage your anxiety as you stroll into your supplemental class. If you're successful, this class could become one of your favorite periods of the day.

42

BREATHE LIKE A NAVY SEAL

I LOVE THE books and podcasts by former Navy SEAL Mark Divine, and I'm inspired by the ordeal that potential Navy SEALS must endure. I can't fathom withstanding cold water for extended periods, but I learned that one of their coping mechanisms is controlled breathing. Mark has minted the label "box breathing" for his version of this technique. It goes like this: breathe in for a four-count, hold your breath for a four-count, exhale for a four-count, and then hold your breath again for a four-count. Repeat. Methodical breathing can help manage panic. I utilize box breathing during workouts and before stressful situations. Try it today before your challenging class or before a meeting with your principal. If you can snatch a bit of calm before such trials, you may find unexpected success.

43

CELEBRATE YOUR
SANCTUARY

IF YOU'VE LIVED long enough, you've experienced a catastrophe. It could be a health issue, the painful end of a relationship, the death of a beloved parent or spouse, or the devastating loss of a child. I've experienced, or dear friends have experienced, each of these tragedies. When they strike, it seems impossible to get out of bed when the alarm erupts. That assumes, however, that you've even slept a wink. But just maybe, getting out of bed and going to school are exactly what you need. Your classroom is a remarkably stable sanctuary. Today, appreciate this anchor. When your world is falling apart, your classroom and your students will be a bedrock of normality. Recognize this anchor as a magnificent asset.

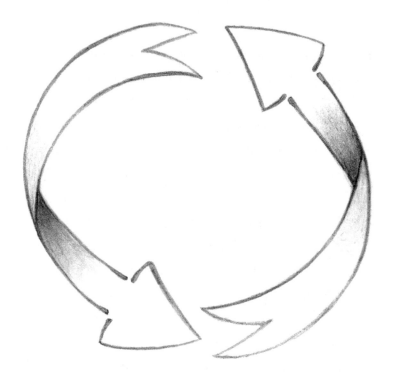

44

GO OUTSIDE

IT WAS LATE March in Ohio. My wife and I were on spring break, and the weather was beautiful. We decided to take a hike, and as Roberta Flack once sang, "Watch winter turn to spring." It was invigorating. It reminded me of one year when I had my planning period the last period of the day. On days when it wasn't raining or snowing or below freezing, which describes a lot of days in Ohio, I would leave school and walk to our stadium. I would then stroll one lap around the track. After my lap, I'd return to my room and be productive. It was awesome. I'm going to start doing that again. Today, carve out fifteen minutes to leave the institutional atmosphere of the school and energize yourself outside.

45

CUT YOURSELF SOME SLACK

I'VE TAUGHT THOUSANDS of students over the course of my career. Guess what? A few of them didn't like me. It certainly wasn't because I didn't try to bond with them, because I did. Something about me must have rubbed them the wrong way. It's sad that we didn't connect, but you're going to have students like that. Today, as you agonize over that kid you've tried everything with, commit to continue trying, but don't take it too hard if it doesn't work out. Just keep trying. Perhaps, if you take some pressure off yourself, they may come around.

46

EXPLORE THE INNER SANCTUM

SOME DAYS IN my planning period, I feel a strong desire to escape. When the weather is bad, and going outside is not an option, I take an indoor excursion. One favorite stop is our school greenhouse in the basement, because it's a magnificent refuge on a rainy day or in the bleakness of an Ohio winter. There's also a small room in the back of the woodshop that I consider as a quiet sanctuary. Taking an indoor stroll also lets you interact with students and colleagues whom you rarely see. Today, during your planning period, go on a brief exploration. You may find somewhere or someone that will enrich your day.

47

IDENTIFY YOUR IDENTITY

WHEN YOU'RE ASKED at a party what you do for a living, do you respond, "I'm a teacher," or do you say, "I teach"? I challenge you to start saying you teach. Embrace the fact that you are not your job. The life expectancy in the U.S. is approaching eighty years. If you teach for thirty years, that does not even represent 40 percent of your life. There was a you before you started teaching, and there will be a you after. Today, begin to internalize the *I teach* paradigm. You'll learn to view yourself as broader than just your job. Because you know what? You are.

48

CLOSE YOUR WINDOWS

EMILY FLETCHER IS a meditation guru. I loved her book *Stress Less Accomplish More.* She likens our minds to computers with numerous minimized windows that are still running in the tab at the bottom of our screens. You may be trying to focus on giving a student valuable feedback, but a lingering concern over your offspring, the decision of what to make for dinner, a frustration with your spouse, or brainstorming ways to squeeze in a workout after school keeps invading your mental space. Today, when you need to focus but find yourself distracted, envision each of your involuntary detours like a program running at the bottom of your screen. Maximize any distraction, "X" out of it, and then turn your attention back to your wonderful students.

49

LAUGH AT A MISTAKE

MY LOVE OF India combined with my awareness that fifteen-year-olds love to move created conditions ripe for my embarrassment. Fridays are a good day to change the classroom routine. One Friday during the India unit, I ushered my class to the gymnasium and led them in several yoga poses. Yes, ninth graders are a lot more flexible than middle-aged men, but they still happily allowed me to guide them. It beat sitting in the classroom. Their joy morphed to unbridled mirth when I rotated from the bridge pose (facing the ceiling) to the down dog pose (hands and feet on the floor and butt in the air) and accidentally unleashed a loud fart. There's nothing a teacher can do in such a situation but to disintegrate into laughter too. It's so important to be authentic with students. Teachers are people, and we do silly things. Be real. Laugh at yourself. Doing so will be of great benefit to you and a shining example of emotional balance for students.

50

PRIORITIZE

WHEN MY MOTHER became terminally ill, it was devastating and stressful. My father had passed several years prior, and my poor mom faced declining health by herself. My siblings, my dear giving wife, and I each took personal days and sick days and spent time with her. Those days began to add up. I began balking at opportunities I could've spent with my mom so I could be at school. Also, when I was with my mom, I often was preoccupied with lessons and grading. I mourn when I think about my priorities during that time. Today, put your family first. Don't elevate a lesson you're preparing, a lesson you won't even remember in a month, over a family member in need.

51

SPLASH AROUND

AN OLD COLLEGE friend used to utter a great line: "That dude is a big fish in a small pond." The colleague you envy so much might be a big deal at your school, but your school is a small universe. Please keep that perspective in mind when you suffer pangs of jealousy. Today, commit to a healthier preoccupation like becoming a better teacher in your classroom with your students. In other words, in your small pond. Also, strive to become a happier teacher, and no longer compare yourself to your local all-stars. You may be in that category one day, but don't obsess over it. Today, just enjoy your small pond.

52

HEED YOUR INNER VOICE

IF YOU'RE INCLINED to say what's on your mind, that natural inclination can get you in trouble. Examples abound of both celebrities and private citizens posting on social media exactly what's on their minds and then suffering dire consequences. Today, remember that whatever you say in class is one student post away from being a national news story. If a powerful, spontaneous, yet controversial idea pops into your head during instruction, postpone its delivery. Give in to your inner voice of reason for twenty-four hours, or at least a period, to render a verdict on its suitability. You could even provide a generic description of your inner struggle and decision to refrain from posting or pontificating. Perhaps your example of restraint will inspire a kid to do the same—and avoid a catastrophe.

53

ELEVATE CIVILITY

OFTEN, TEACHERS ARE in a rush to get ready for class. Once the starting gun erupts for the day, K–12 educators can feel overwhelmed with the constant presence of students, sometimes up to 150 students who surge at them in waves of thirty each period. It's understandable if the HyperDoc for your third period class has a typo. But this unfortunate error could be an opportunity. Today, empower students to find your mistakes and then challenge them to inform you of your errors in a respectful and positive way. Don't reward David if he blurts it out in the middle of the period. Allow students to help you become a better teacher and encourage civility in the process.

54

LOOK OUT THE WINDOW

THE WINDOWS IN my room face due east and provide a prime perspective on the dense forest beside our school. My room is like an observation deck that affords a marvelous visual journey through nature's yearly cycle. In October, the sun filters through red and gold maples. In December, the sun turns the sky pink, and you can see it clearly through the dormant trees as it inches over the horizon. Then in May, the sun is higher and shines brightly above the lush forest. Today, be one of a handful of teachers in the long history of education to encourage students to look out the window.

55

DO ALGEBRA

IT'S DIFFICULT NOT to take student negativity personally. You work hard to prepare for class. If you're excited about the lesson, yet the kids seem bored and dismissive, it hurts. I recently conducted a structured class discussion on an engaging topic. A few of my reliable participants broadcast negative nonverbal messages. They didn't participate much, looked bored, and one all-star contributor even put her head down for a stretch. I was frustrated, but I later learned that she was mostly upset by a classmate who made valid points to oppose her position. I was not part of the equation. Today, keep in mind that students are complicated, and a negative reaction to your lesson may come down to numerous subtle variables that have nothing to do with you.

56

BE VULNERABLE

THREE OF THE most powerful words in the English language are "I need help." It's okay to be vulnerable. Insecure people are often afraid to show vulnerability and ask for help. However, there's great power in admitting deficiencies. Today, ask a colleague for fresh ideas on how you might teach a lesson that has become stale. Or inquire about a new approach to dealing with a challenging student. You could even ask how they stay so fit or remain so positive. Allow them to come to your rescue. Empower others by asking for help, and in the process, demonstrate your humility. You may discover awesome solutions.

57

CLOSE YOUR DOOR

DURING A BUSY school day, do you ever feel like you're swimming in people? Your classes are big, the halls are packed, the lunch room is a sea of humanity, and the parking lot is a bottleneck. And to top it off, you desperately have to use the facilities between periods, so you hustle down to the bathroom in the faculty lounge only to find it occupied, the door locked. You need a break! Teachers are givers, but how about today, for just one period, being a taker? Check to see if any student needs you during your planning period. If none do, close the door, turn out the lights, and meditate, or look at the internet, or watch stupid videos, or buy something on Amazon, and allow the world outside your door to evaporate.

58

GO HOME

SOME TEACHERS ARE martyrs about stress. They broadcast how much they have to do even when they haven't been prompted. Today, do the opposite of that. Before you exit the building, make sure that your room is neat and ready to roll for tomorrow's first period. And then walk out the door. From the moment you leave school today until you return tomorrow morning, do absolutely nothing pertaining to school. Try not to even think about it. It'll be good for you and even better for your family.

59

DON'T TAKE THE BAIT

AS A TEACHER, recognize that sometimes you get played. There's harmless manipulation when students talk you into postponing an assignment for a day. And then there's more diabolical manipulation when a kid intentionally attempts to make you look bad. I once had an oppositional student who'd try to bait me into arguments. Early in the semester, I made the mistake of accepting one of his invitations. Thankfully, after that experience, I recognized his obsession with controlling social situations. I stopped falling into the traps he set, and the atmosphere in my class and my relationship with the provocateur improved. Today, recognize when students are manipulating you. It may be harmless, but try not to be a puppet. Calmly avoiding this type of manipulation puts you back in control and your important lesson back on course.

60

HIDE ENCOURAGEMENTS

LAST SEMESTER, I had a tough geography class. It was populated by a host of freshman football players, who were far more interested in messing with each other than they were in the five geographic themes. I assigned a complex project. Halfway through the instructions, I'd lost them. I got frustrated and raised my voice. That was counterproductive, and I felt silly. Before our next project, I wrote encouragements on Post-it notes and stuck them in locations only I could see. I wrote things like, *Dominic will get frustrated by the instructions,* and *This crew will take longer to get on task, but they'll get there.* It helped me manage my frustrations and create a better classroom atmosphere. It was my little secret, which made it fun. Today, create Post-it note messages to help you through your challenging class.

SECTION 4

MAGENTA TEACHERS ADAPT

SPECIES, MICROORGANISMS, BUSINESSES, sports franchises, artists, metropolitan areas, nations, and entertainers all must adapt to survive. (This is an extremely short and merely representative list.) Any rational person understands the critical necessity for all things and all carbon-based life-forms, educators included, to evolve. Schools today certainly are different than the schools of our youth. This is true even for young teachers. The world is changing rapidly. That's why, in this section, we'll explore the dispositions of flexibility, suppleness, openness, and adaptability. When an educator embraces adaptability, they'll undermine any future label of being the grumpy old teacher at the end of the hall who desperately needs to retire. Instead, they'll be a role model of openness and relevancy to both students and colleagues.

61

BE INCONSISTENT

TEACHERS FREQUENTLY ARE encouraged to be consistent in terms of grades and classroom management. But humanity is certainly diverse. Today, venture into variability, and teach each period differently. You could opt for diverse venues. Take one period to the cafeteria, another to the library, and another outside. Try a different lesson hook with each period. Each class, alter your lesson plan slightly—or fundamentally. In one class, conduct direct instruction. In another, unleash student-led learning. You could allow kids to design the lesson and how you will deliver it. Or introduce randomness by prompting students to make a blind choice like a roll of the dice or a coin flip. You may find a magnificent way to teach a lesson.

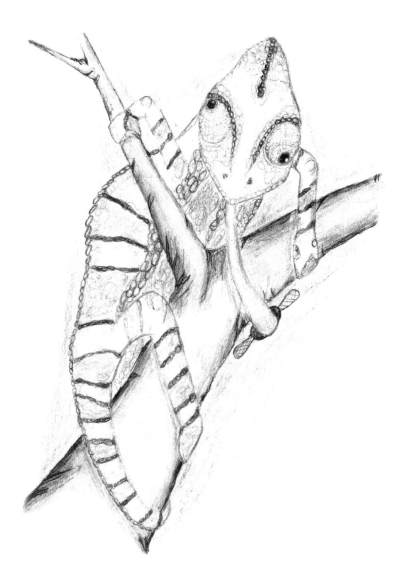

62

KEEP TINKERING

YOU PROBABLY HAVE a favorite meal, but if you ate it every day, you'd get tired of it. What's true of menus is true of teaching strategies. I'm a huge fan of structured class discussions with strategies such as Socratic Seminars and Philosophical Chairs, but late in the year, student performance and engagement would peak with these tactics. By May, the law of diminishing returns reared its ugly head. That is exactly the time to start tinkering. That's when I utilized the tech platform Plickers and a small-group discussion strategy called Talking Sticks. Both strategies were refreshing. Today, start tinkering. Your go-to teaching strategy might be hitting on all cylinders now, but as the year drags on, it may become less reliable. Evolve and try something new.

63

PLUNGE INTO THE FOUNTAIN OF YOUTH

TEACHING CAN MAKE you feel old. Your students listen to unfamiliar music, wear bizarre clothes, play foreign computer games, have smooth skin, sport full heads of hair, display slim waistlines, and manipulate arthritis-free joints. It's easy to be envious. Today, shelve this envy and allow students to act as your remarkable Fountain of Youth. You can learn from them by asking or just observing. Better yet, invite them to teach you their culture. Do this regularly and then amaze your contemporaries at neighborhood parties with your grasp of contemporary youth culture, even if you demonstrate this awareness while wearing mom jeans or dad shoes.

64

SCULPT THE ROCK

TEACHING IS A massively humbling experience. When I teach a unit on Taoism in my world civilization class, students learn that this ancient faith discourages battling against powerful forces. Instead of struggling against such forces, Taoists learn to accommodate them. Once they do that, they can impact the world. Consider water and rock. The hard, inflexible rock directs the course of the water in a stream, but over the eons, the water sculpts the rock. Today, be like the subtle water. Don't fight so hard against criticisms and setbacks. Accommodate them and learn from the barbs. This is not a sign of weakness. Critical students—and colleagues—can teach you a lot about how to become a magnificent teacher.

65

RAKE THE GRAVEL

JAPANESE GARDENS ARE populated with beautifully manicured gravel areas. These areas are like sand traps on golf courses, and they frequently are raked in beautiful patterns. The resulting sculpted ridges and shaped gravel resemble gentle waves. Today, rake the gravel areas in your lesson. Change it up, and give your class a whole new flow.

66

RECOGNIZE AN OPPORTUNITY

YOUR DAY IS probably remarkably predictable. You wake up at the same time, you adhere to your class schedule that seems to be chiseled in stone, and you eat lunch at the same location with the same people who talk about the same things. This daily scenario may seem to enforce rigidity and conformity, but hold on! I've always felt liberated by this. Change your way of looking at it. Instead of routine, make your schedule an opportunity. Routines allow you to relinquish control over certain aspects of planning. Instead of zoning out, use that free mental time to experiment with other aspects of instruction. You do not have to focus on your commute or your lunch-time conversation, so why not use the time to develop new lesson plans or a new way to involve kids in the classroom?

67

TAKE A COLD SHOWER

WHEN YOU FIRST turn on the shower, it takes a moment for the hot water to migrate through the pipes. As you cower and wait in the corner, frigid drops and spray torment you. Finally, the hot water emerges, and you catch a glimpse of Nirvana. Teaching is like showering. Until students warm up to you, they can be pretty frigid and pelt you with discomfort. Today, when you're luxuriating in the warmth of your shower, briefly turn the water on cold. See if you can calm yourself amid this icy onslaught. Breathe deeply and understand that you're in no danger. It may take numerous attempts before you can calmly handle this assault to your senses. But once you do, you'll think about the practice the next time a cantankerous kid throws cold water all over your lesson. You'll simply breathe deeply and acknowledge that the discomfort is temporary, and the glorious warmth will return soon and will feel awesome.

68

ERADICATE FUSSINESS

ARE YOU FUSSY? If you are, try to stop! Fussy people are annoying, and being an annoying teacher can be a problem. It's appropriate and necessary to be annoying when you're trying to help students fulfill their obligations, but being annoying becomes an issue when it's about trivial things. If the copier breaks, or your projector bulb burns out, or the office interrupts class with an announcement, or your favorite team loses, these obstacles are the stuff of everyday existence. It's a shame if you allow them to ruin your day. Your students are in no way responsible and certainly do not deserve to experience your wrath. Expect something annoying to happen to you today. Don't fuss. Instead, just roll with it. Your students will be grateful.

69

ESCAPE THE AMBER

I'M CERTAIN MANY students think their teachers are suspended in amber like prehistoric insects. If a teacher graduated from high school in 1990, that educator is stuck in the past if they attempt to revive the styles of that era by continuing to don their favorite get-up in hopes it will become hip again. It's darn near impossible to keep up with youth trends, but today, give it a shot. You certainly don't have to dress like your kids, but find some aspect of contemporary youth culture, and embrace it. I love the old people's social media platform, but recently I started posting on a platform favored by modern youth. My students were delighted with my efforts and showed me the ropes. I like the old people platform better, but what the heck. Letting my students school me was a fun bonding experience, and it broke me out of my amber tomb.

70

ENTER THE LABORATORY

EINSTEIN QUIPPED, "INSANITY is doing the same thing over and over and expecting different results." You probably have recurring frustrations with a class or with certain students. If these problems are indeed recurring, revisit Einstein's quote. Instead of expecting different results when you use the same failed tactics, become the change agent. It never fails to amaze me when frustrated teachers bitterly complain about students but cannot point to many examples of how they've approached instruction or classroom management differently. Today, try a new approach. Tomorrow, try another one. Keep experimenting until one of your ideas gains traction.

71

JUXTAPOSE YOUR FAVORITE NOVEL

I LOVED DOUGLAS Adams's *The Hitchhiker's Guide to the Galaxy.* I read it in college, and it made me laugh and brought me joy, and I couldn't wait to read a chapter at bedtime as I drifted off into unconsciousness. In that silly, marvelous, creative book, Adams inserts humor in places where it doesn't seem to belong. Following his example, I decided to add humor into lessons at junctures where it didn't seem to fit. The class suddenly became more interesting for everyone. Today, consider your favorite novel. It thoroughly engaged you, or you wouldn't have read it. Try to take an aspect of that novel and juxtapose it onto today's lesson. Transform your class into a page-turner.

72

BECOME THE STUDENT
YOU WANT TO TEACH

"BE THE CHANGE you want to see in the world" is one of Gandhi's most shared quotes. However, this directive is at odds with the often-stated cliché concerning teachers: "Teachers make the worst students." I've witnessed this phenomenon as I've sat through decades of faculty meetings and presented at scores of professional development sessions. At today's faculty meeting, be authentic and involved. Conduct yourself as you would like students to participate in your class. Maybe you'll hear about an idea that will transform your teaching. This happens to me when I listen with an open mind—like a good student.

73

RELINQUISH THE RED PEN

WHEN I WAS a student, and a teacher returned my research paper, I was primarily concerned with my grade. If I got a B, I was cool with that, and I stuffed it in my bookbag and never gave it a second thought. Once I became a teacher, I understood the supreme frustration my former instructors felt when they filled the margins of my paper with detailed instructions on how I could become a better writer, only to have me largely ignore it. Today, embrace what research claims is a powerful learning tactic. Give students the rubric and have them assess their own work. Then challenge them to make revisions.

74

CLEAR A PATH

ALLOW WHAT YOU teach to impact how you interact with the world in a highly visible and demonstrative way. At one point, my class was studying the Chinese concept of chi. Chi is the invisible flow of energy through living things, geographic features, and even human-made structures. If chi is blocked in the body, interventions like tai chi or acupuncture can free it. Feng shui is a way of healing an indoor space by rearranging furniture to stimulate the flow of chi. At one point in my lesson on chi, I gazed around the room and told my students, "This room is a mess. Let's feng shui it." We got rid of a lot of things and rearranged. It was fun and helped us create a more energetic classroom. Students felt inspired to do the same in their rooms at home, so I made it a homework assignment. It was popular with moms—and it worked because I was taking a more flexible teaching approach, rather than staying stuck.

75

MIX AND MATCH

CHANGE YOUR SEATING chart to foster new relationships and provide kids with new perspectives. There are unlimited ways to sort students. You can arrange them in alphabetical order, but try doing it by first or middle names. Arrange them chronologically in terms of birth order on the calendar, from January to December babies. You could even arrange them based on their favorite movies, oldest to newest. Today, rearrange your seating chart. Take your class into the hall, describe the sorting factor, and challenge them to figure out the order.

76

BREAK OUT THE BROOM

I USED TO despise lunch duty. It was gross. Watching fifteen-year-olds eat was enough to make me embark on a hunger strike. Then, one day during my planning period, I needed to find my friend and colleague Kevin Ellinwood. He just so happened to be on his lunch duty. When I entered the cafeteria, I was amazed at Kevin's markedly different approach to this obligation. Instead of sulking in the corner, trying not to get hit with shrapnel, he was out amongst the masses with a broom and dustpan. He was having fun cleaning up after the kids and interacting with them. His example transformed me. I followed his lead and then began to *enjoy* lunch duty. Today, adapt your attitude about a tedious duty.

77

HUNT FOR A MENTOR

YOUR STUDENTS CAN help you grow as an educator if you let them. Within twenty-four hours, a student demonstrated to me a neat way to utilize transitions in Google Slides. Another kid showed me an app that erases backgrounds on images. This ability will help me transform many of my favorite images, which I'd like to utilize in presentations. I loved what these two students unveiled to me. Today, challenge your students to teach *you* something. Your directive might not bring immediate results, but you'll plant seeds that will one day germinate. In the process, you'll demonstrate to students that you respect them.

78

SHIFT GEARS

WHEN I WAS sixteen, I learned to drive a standard transmission. It was frustrating at first. I lived in a town with steep hills, and if you got stopped at a traffic light and your car was aimed uphill, things got real! When learning to drive a stick, you have to listen to and feel the engine. When it starts to strain, it's time to shift. After some initial frustration, I quickly mastered driving a car with a clutch and a stick. Today, monitor students like you're learning to drive a standard transmission. Listen to them, observe their body language, and feel for when their enthusiasm starts to wane. Then it's time to shift gears and teach in a different fashion. With practice, you'll become an expert in knowing when it's time to change tactics.

79

APPROACH THE BOSS

YOUR TEACHER EVALUATION is on the near horizon. It's understandable if you want to put on a great show. You might lean on a reliable lesson that's worked in the past or a favorite teaching technique that you've employed to perfection. Instead, decide where your instruction is weak and then tell your principal that you want to grow in this area and that you'd like their help. They'll probably greet your idea with enthusiasm. Take all the resources they provide (hopefully, some are human), and craft a lesson that will demonstrate your evolution. This could be a transformational evaluation for you and your principal.

80

TWEAK SOMETHING

RIGIDITY IS BAD. Suppleness is good. Last year, I was excited to shepherd kids through a unit review that mimicked the classic board game Clue. I thought it would be an epic experience for all. However, right out of the chute, first period, I learned that it wasn't. The students had to check their answers before they could advance in the game. There was only one key, and I had it, so a huge bottleneck formed as students waited for me to check their answers so they could advance in the game. In second period, I made changes, and the lesson improved. By the last period, I gave a number of answer keys to student helpers stationed throughout the room. My lesson idea morphed into a powerful learning activity, but it sure didn't start that way. Today, be supple and make adjustments to your lesson each period.

SECTION 5

MAGENTA TEACHERS FIND CONTENTMENT

WHEN I REFLECT on my time as both a teacher and a student, the memories that erupt are the moments of raucous laughter, the surprises, the incredible relationships, and the deep feelings of accomplishment. These were moments of pure contentment. Sure, everyone has miserable memories, too. Unfortunately, some students—and teachers—had largely negative academic experiences. But that's not what we're about right now.

Your task in traversing this section is to be empowered to create positive memories for your students. Inspire them to look back on your class fondly, even generations from now. This is a wonderful way to conclude this book because it has the potential for deep transformation. In this section, you may be inspired to notice things that need changing—but you also may learn that contentment is right under your nose, and you're too preoccupied to notice. This is not only a path to becoming a happier teacher but also a path to profound fulfillment.

81

RAISE YOUR VOICE

I ONCE HAD a colleague who was pretty good-natured. As I was walking by his room one day, I heard him getting angry. I remember him bellowing, "There are teachers in this building who raise their voice every day, and I'm not one of them! That should tell you something!" He was right. He rarely raised his voice, but that was a missed opportunity. You don't have to be mad to raise your voice. Be ecstatic when a student succeeds. Demonstrate unbridled joy. Erupt in pride at a kid's achievement.

James Alan Sturtevant

82

CHANNEL THE INNER FIVE-YEAR-OLD

WHEN YOU WERE a little kid, your momma would give you paper and crayons, and you'd be set for the next thirty minutes. You nodded with pride as you slammed down your crayon, and then delivered your masterpiece to your mother, who lavished praise as she posted it on the fridge. Unfortunately, the next year you went to kindergarten and started comparing your drawing to those of your peers. Your art no longer seemed so special. As you matriculated through elementary and middle school, you lost your artistic enthusiasm and confidence. Today, bring that childlike artistic bravery back. Tell students this story and challenge them to draw something pertaining to your lesson. You draw, too. You may transport the entire room back to the creative confidence of age five.

83

PLAY SWEET JAMS

A LOT OF folks play music to add joy to tedious tasks. I hate to call your class tedious, but the entire school day is tedious for some kids. To combat monotony, add joy into today's lesson by adding a soundtrack. Play it at a low level as your kids morph into creation mode. Your students may have questions about your playlist, and you can explain why you selected a particular song, what impact you hope the song will have, and why this song is meaningful to you. You'll not only soothe the savage beast with music but become more interesting to your students.

84

SAY HELLO

TEACHING CAN BE a rough job, particularly if the kids aren't nice to you. One action you can take today is to simply smile and say "Hello" to every kid you pass in the hallway. If you teach at a large school, many of the students may be unfamiliar. Turn this activity into a game. See how many kids respond. It may be under half. Don't sweat this at all. Just smile and greet the next young face. The mere action of smiling and saying "hi" will put you in a better mood and demonstrate to the entire student body that friendly teachers are in their midst. If you do this often, some kids, even those you don't know, may beat you to the punch and offer a greeting before you can unleash yours.

85

GREET A FIFTY-YEAR-OLD

IF TEACHERS ARE honest with themselves, they'll admit that many of the lessons they enthusiastically teach every day will not create a lasting impact on students. Conversely, the relationships they forge with students, whether negative or positive, tend to last. Keep that in mind today. The way you treat students will ultimately make more of an impact than your content. Consequently, strive to treat students with extra kindness, empathy, respect, and love. It was humbling and rewarding when a fifty-year-old man approached me and said, "Hey, Mr. Sturtevant, do you remember me? I used to be in your class." I doubt if he remembered any of my lesson plans, but he sure remembered me. That's powerful. Treat your students the way you want them to remember you when they are fifty.

86

TELL A STORY

PEOPLE HAVE TOLD stories for as long as there've been words. Each of the world's major faith traditions utilizes stories to convey important ideas. In the classroom, stories bring dull lessons to life. This book contains many stories that work as hooks, help explain concepts, and give practical examples. Today, tell a story that will inspire students about the day's lesson. It could be how you, or perhaps a famous person, interacted with the lesson topic. Or it could be an abstract allegory. This is a challenging prompt, but the potential payoff is highly engaged students.

87

TELL A JOKE

HUMOR IS A wonderful classroom engagement tool. I once told a ten-minute-long joke about the French Revolution. The Jacobins were preparing to execute an engineer on the guillotine. It malfunctioned. The engineer, unable to contain himself, diagnosed the problem with the guillotine, and promptly fixed it. Then they executed him with the repaired device. I stretched out this ridiculous joke for ten minutes by acting out many of the parts. Students commented on this joke decades later. That's the engagement power of humor. Today, tell a joke about the unit you're studying. It may be ridiculous, and few, if any, kids might laugh, but I say go for it! If this directive paralyzes you, deputize a funny kid in your class to find a joke for you. They won't let you down.

88

REMEMBER WHAT THEY'LL REMEMBER

SURE, YOUR KIDS may do well on their ACT and come back and thank you for preparing them. You may have one lesson that engaged them, which they'll bring up when you run into them at the grocery in a decade. But I'll wager that what they'll most remember about you is the way you treated them. Yes, they'll be grateful you helped them master an academic skill or content, but how you supported them, the kindness and patience you demonstrated, and the humor you utilized to cheer them up and give them confidence have the real shelf life. Keep that in mind today before you cut short a conversation with a student.

89

SHOW YOUR PALMS

THROUGH MY STUDY of nonverbal communication, I've learned that a great way to put others at ease is to display the empty palms of my hands. It's like saying to those you're attempting to greet, "Look, I'm not carrying any weapons. You've nothing to fear." The first time I was exposed to this idea, I laughed intermittently for a full hour. I greeted every student at school the next day with this open palm gesture. Most of the kids were curious, which offered me the opportunity to explain and perhaps initiate a relationship or forge a deeper one. Today, think of a curious way to greet students. You could greet them in another language or mimic a welcoming gesture from another culture. Hopefully, they'll inquire about it and present you with an opportunity to explain.

90

UNLEASH YOUR ADRENALINE

IF YOU'RE ENTHUSIASTIC about today's lesson (I hope you are), communicate that by demonstrating excitement. How can you possibly expect kids to be enthusiastic when you don't appear to be? How you accomplish this is as unique to you as your fingerprints, so express it in your special way. You may find that your kids are a reflection of you. When shown how pumped you are for today's lesson, they might follow suit.

91

ASK FOR THE MENU

FOOD AND I go way back. Most people feel the same. It's amazing how many TV shows are devoted solely to the preparation and consumption of food. The massive nature of American restaurant portions also demonstrates the importance food plays in our lives. I credit math teacher Mark Robinson with teaching me this brilliant bonding trick. As soon as he shared this idea with me, I started using it. Periodically, ask students what they had last night for dinner. In the process, you'll learn a lot about your kids' home lives and perhaps also sponsor enjoyable convo, not just with you, but with peers who overhear and then are intrigued enough to issue their own meal report. All of this food-inspired fellowship will foster contentment not only in you but also your students.

92

CIRCULATE

WAYNE MOORE WAS one of my favorite colleagues. He retired about a decade ago, and I think of him often. He was one of those guys who walked around the building and interacted with people, often poking his head into a room just to say hello. He didn't distract you from prepping for a class because he only monopolized your attention for a matter of seconds, but you knew he was there, and that he cared. Wayne is a role model for me. When I cruise around my building and greet people, it seems to make them feel good. Many aren't satisfied with a simple greeting, so they draw me into an enjoyable conversation. This is how you create a magical working environment. Today, get out of your room to circulate and greet your colleagues.

93

PASS OUT PAPERS

SO MANY MISSED opportunities take place in the school day. You may already interact with kids when they enter and leave your room, or in the hallway between periods, or during your duty. But many teachers shift gears in their classrooms and don't look for opportunities to engage with students. Instead, they're all business when the bell rings. Today, utilize the simple task of passing out papers. Instead of warp speed, slow it down. Navigate the room, lingering at each student's desk. Initiate friendly banter with each kid, and make sure it has nothing to do with school. Savor each interaction. Before you know it, the semester will be over, and you may never see these kids again. Leave an impression by making sure that you took advantage of seeing them when you could.

94

TEAM UP

MY CLASSROOM IS Room 111, and it's a self-contained universe. At times, it feels like I teach in the isolated Room 111 Local School District. However, some of my most successful lessons have included the participation of colleagues. This participation could've been in the creation phase, but I'm more interested in the lesson's delivery phase. Today, invite a colleague from their planning period to join your students. Your esteemed guest could be part of a Socratic Seminar or join a student group tasked with a challenge. No matter what, make sure they are part of the learning process. It's good for students to see teachers as collaborators.

95

BECOME A REALTOR

I ARRANGED THE desks in my room so the center was open like a Greek Agora, where the action took place. My desk was off to one side, and a few student desks were close to mine. I often reshuffled my seating chart, and consequently, frequently got new neighbors, sometimes by design and at other times through random chance. Regardless, my objective was to focus my bonding efforts on the kids close to my desk when I was stationed there. If you alter your seating chart frequently, you can give yourself lots of new neighbors. Today, engage in small talk with a student who sits close to you. You might make a new friend.

96

DESCRIBE A MISTAKE

TOO FREQUENTLY, WHEN I tell a story, I come off as the hero. This makes me uncomfortable. I'm more at ease when I describe making a mistake and learning from it. Here's an example: I was referred to Dr. Kwame Osei, an endocrinologist at Ohio State University Hospital, to evaluate my thyroid condition. My initial reaction to the referral was, *Oh, he's from Nigeria. Are the medical schools there as good as the ones in the U.S.?* He turned out to be a magnificent doctor, and my initial reaction was pure stereotyping. I retell this story every year to introduce a lesson on stereotyping. Please don't hesitate to tell such stories where you're not the hero. Your students will respect your authenticity and learn from your mistakes.

97

FIND YOUR GURU

KRISTIN SPAYDE IS my guru. She is also thirty years younger than me. A decade ago, I wasn't open to asking younger colleagues for guidance. I was accustomed to them coming to me and thought that was the way it should be. A couple of years ago, during a breakout session at a faculty meeting, Kristin was in my small discussion group. She expertly described how she utilized a tech tool. I sought her out after the meeting and asked for guidance, then successfully employed her idea. I've been hitting her up for ideas ever since. Today, get over yourself and go seek out a younger colleague, and ask for help or an idea. They'll feel valued, and you'll be inspired to try something new.

98

BROADCAST LESS

MY WIFE USED to be a middle school principal, and she got a lot of phone calls, most of which could've been shorter. Talking too long is rude. Unfortunately, some teachers do it daily. Think about TED Talks, where presenters have eighteen minutes to make their point. And some of their points are darned complex. Now, ask yourself, *Do I drone on too long? Can I respect my students more and get to the point?* It doesn't mean that you can't include humor and segments where you venture off on verbal detours. It just means that you must manage how much time you monopolize the airwaves. Today, decide what message you want to communicate and then determine how to deliver it more concisely. You'll maintain your students' focus—and their respect.

99

BE AUTHENTIC

I DECIDED TO get my teaching license at age twenty-three. That was late in my college academic career. I worked on it on the side as I navigated through obtaining my M.A. in history from Ohio State. I was assigned to a suburban middle school to complete student teaching, and in the midst of it, I wasn't sure I liked teaching. I kept trying to mimic my cooperating teacher. It didn't feel natural, because we were different people in terms of temperament and objectives. Fortunately, I was successful in my job search following student teaching. I hoped that once I had my own class, I could follow my instincts and thrive. My wish came true. Today, feel free to borrow ideas from successful colleagues, but make certain to celebrate your unique instructional fingerprint. It's who you are.

100
DO A CHEER

SCHOOLS ARE SMALL communities. As a teacher, you're a VIP in this little universe. As such, show some patriotism. Today, celebrate a school achievement, gush over a student's extracurricular triumph, pull on your school gear, and when the opportunity presents itself, speak highly of your school. When students witness your enthusiasm, they're more likely to express school spirit. Schools with spirit are great places to teach, and more importantly, they're great places to learn.

CONCLUSION
APPROACHING MAGENTA

WHEN I WAS in grade school, I used to stare at the clock before recess, hoping it would hurry up. I fixated on the minute hand, watching it move ever so slowly in tiny increments. Then the teacher would notice my trance and crab at me to pay attention. After a bit of involuntary and probably necessary distraction, I'd sneak a glance back at the clock ... and invariably notice that the minute hand had moved a lot! It amazed me how small, subtle changes, like the slow march of the minute hand, magically added up to big changes, like time for recess, particularly if I wasn't constantly looking for the change.

Maybe you've had a similar experience matriculating through this book. Perhaps, unbeknownst to you, you've changed a lot in the small steps we've been taking. You may have read a page or two daily starting in September, and now it's cold out. You may have started in February, and now you're composing your final exams. Regardless of your pace, my great hope is that this book changed you. Like when I was a little kid and got surprised when I glanced back at the clock and saw that it was time for recess, perhaps you've evolved to teaching in magenta.

Maybe, to your surprise, students and colleagues are suddenly pointing out just how purplish-red or mauvish-crimson you've become.

If so, congratulations! Welcome to the club, and enjoy your new *Teaching in Magenta* moments!

ABOUT THE AUTHOR

JAMES STURTEVANT navigated thirty-four years in a public high school classroom. He now teaches Intro to Education and Assessment to future teachers at Muskingum University. He combines fearless experimentation with a willingness to learn from younger tech-savvy students and colleagues. He's authored three additional books that promote student engagement and bonding with kids. James hosts the *Hacking Engagement Podcast*, which provides educators with tips, tools, and tactics that teachers can utilize imme-diately. His blog posts have appeared in *Principal Leadership*, *Edutopia*, and *HuffPost*.

James is married to Penny Sturtevant, a fellow edu-cator, and they live in Galena, Ohio. They have three children and two grandchildren. He relishes his role as a classroom teacher and works to keep his perspec-tive fresh, authentic, enthusiastic, and relevant.

ABOUT THE ILLUSTRATOR

LAUREN BARNES is an honors art student, actor, and singer who has performed in dozens of plays and show choir events in and around northeast Ohio. She enjoys writing, playing cards, walking, and spending time with her family. Lauren hopes to continue her art studies in college and plans to travel in the coming years.

ACKNOWLEDGMENTS

A FEW CHRISTMASES ago, my daughter-in-law Niki bought me a book. It was a small volume by the Vietnamese Zen master Thich Nhat Hanh entitled *How to Walk*. As I mentioned in Path 24, I thought the gift was cool, but it didn't make a huge impression. It wasn't like I immediately isolated myself and dove into its pages. Instead, it sat by my desk unopened until spring break. Then, one mellow morning when I wasn't required to bolt out the door and make it to school before my bus duty, it caught my eye, and I casually opened it.

I was instantly intrigued because each page taught a lesson about walking mindfully. Each lesson was short—a couple of paragraphs. Each short narrative encouraged the reader to walk mindfully through one of life's various challenges. I read a page and applied the directives that day. It was a joy! The next day, I read another page and applied it. That's all it took. I was hooked. I was impressed with how little time it took to consume each page, but the directives were powerful and profoundly impacted me. I also loved the rough sketches that accompanied many of the narratives. I thought to myself, *Wouldn't it be cool to write a book like this?*

Consequently, I'd like to acknowledge the potential of a humble gift. My dear daughter-in-law had no idea that her thoughtful present would inspire me to write this book. If this book inspires you to manifest magenta in your classroom, you'll be providing your students with a wonderful humble gift. The initial impact may not be profound, but be patient. Who knows what may evolve from this effort?

MORE FROM
TIMES 10

Browse our library at 10Publications.com

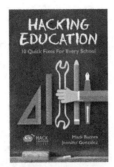

Browse our library at 10Publications.com

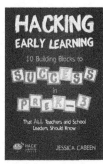

Browse our library at 10Publications.com

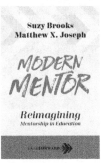

Browse our library at 10Publications.com

Resources from Times 10

10Publications.com

Join the Times 10 Ambassadors and help us revolutionize education:
10Publications.com/ambassador

Podcasts:
hacklearningpodcast.com
jamesalansturtevant.com/podcast

On Twitter:
@10Publications
@HackMyLearning
#Times10News
@LeadForward2
#LeadForward
#HackLearning
#HackingLeadership
#MakeWriting
#HackingQs
#HackingSchoolDiscipline
#LeadWithGrace
#QuietKidsCount
#ModernMentor
#AnxiousBook

All things Times 10:
10Publications.com

Vision, Experience, Action
10PUBLICATIONS.COM

TIMES 10 is helping all education stakeholders improve every aspect of teaching and learning. We are committed to solving big problems with simple ideas. We bring you content from experts, shared through books, podcasts, and an array of social networks. Our books bring Vision, Experience, and Action to educators around the world. Stay in touch with us at 10Publications.com and follow our updates on Twitter @10Publications and #Times10News.

Made in the USA
Monee, IL
23 April 2022